Creative PIANO SOLO

BOHEMIAN RHAPSODY & OTHER EPIC SONGS

Unique, Distinctive Piano Arrangements of 20 Hit Songs

ISBN 978-1-4950-7450-9

7777 W. BLUEMOUND RD. P.O. BOX 13819 MILWAUKEE, WI 53213

Visit Hal Leonard Online at
www.halleonard.com

AQUALUNG

Words and Music by IAN ANDERSON
and JENNIE ANDERSON

To Coda ⊕

Suddenly faster

BABA O'RILEY

Words and Music by
PETER TOWNSHEND

BAND ON THE RUN

Words and Music by PAUL McCARTNEY
and LINDA McCARTNEY

Suddenly faster

BOHEMIAN RHAPSODY

Words and Music by
FREDDIE MERCURY

DEACON BLUES

Words and Music by WALTER BECKER
and DONALD FAGEN

Moderate Swing

D.S. al Coda

CODA

COME SAIL AWAY

Words and Music by
DENNIS DeYOUNG

To Coda ⊕

COMFORTABLY NUMB

Words and Music by ROGER WATERS
and DAVID GILMOUR

To Coda ⊕

A DAY IN THE LIFE

Words and Music by JOHN LENNON
and PAUL McCARTNEY

FREE BIRD

Words and Music by ALLEN COLLINS
and RONNIE VAN ZANT

42

GOOD VIBRATIONS

Words and Music by BRIAN WILSON
and MIKE LOVE

GOLDEN SLUMBERS/ CARRY THAT WEIGHT/ THE END

Words and Music by JOHN LENNON
and PAUL McCARTNEY

Slowly, with feeling

JESSICA

Words and Music by
DICKEY BETTS

To Coda ⊕

LIVE AND LET DIE

Words and Music by PAUL McCARTNEY
and LINDA McCARTNEY

ROUNDABOUT

Words and Music by JON ANDERSON
and STEVE HOWE

FOREPLAY/LONG TIME

Words and Music by
TOM SCHOLZ

Quickly

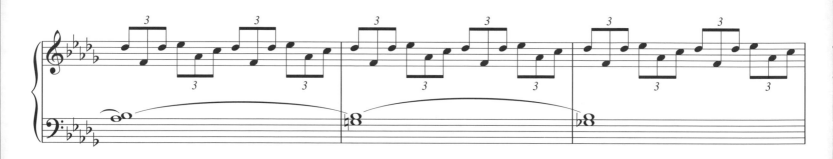

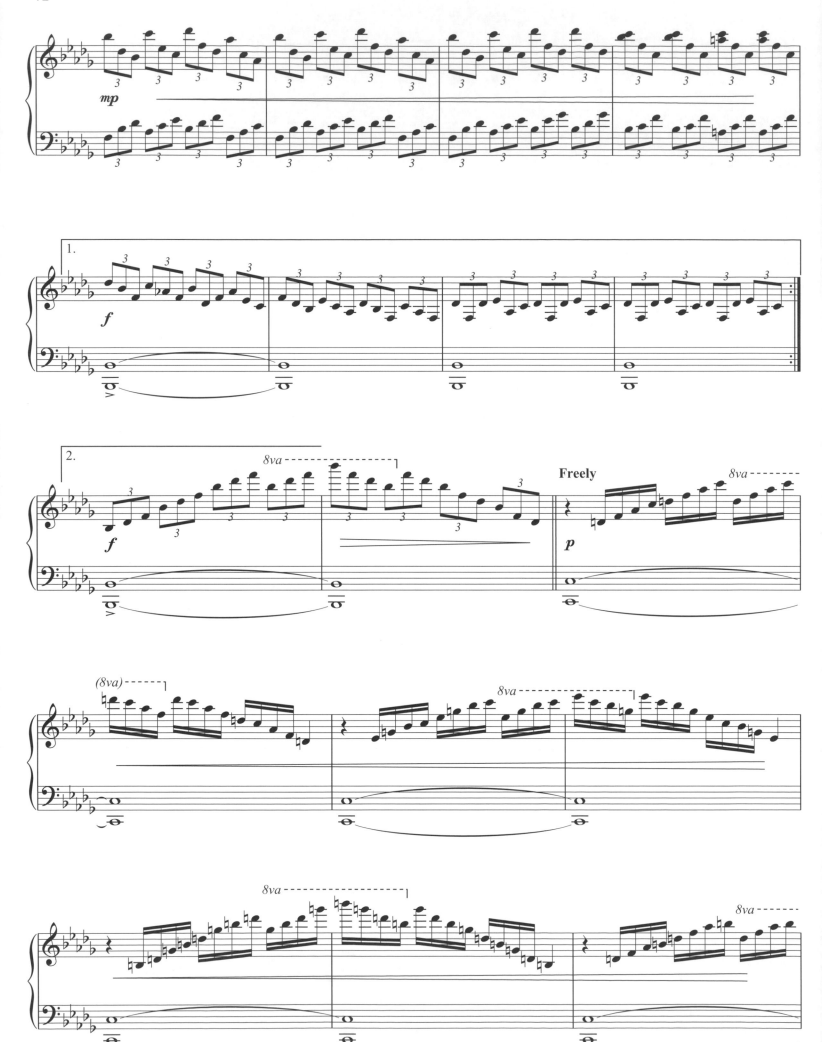

NOVEMBER RAIN

Words and Music by
W. AXL ROSE

PARADISE BY THE DASHBOARD LIGHT

Words and Music by
JIM STEINMAN

PIANO MAN

Words and Music by
BILLY JOEL

Dreamy

STAIRWAY TO HEAVEN

Words and Music by JIMMY PAGE
and ROBERT PLANT

TAKE THE LONG WAY HOME

Words and Music by RICK DAVIES
and ROGER HODGSON

Slowly, in two

Creative PIANO SOLO

Looking to add some variety to your playing? Enjoy these beautifully distinctive arrangements for piano solo! These popular tunes get new and unique treatments for a fun and fresh presentation. Explore new styles and enjoy these favorites with a bit of a twist! Each collection includes 20 songs for the intermediate to advanced player.

BOHEMIAN RHAPSODY & OTHER EPIC SONGS
Band on the Run • A Day in the Life • Free Bird • November Rain • Piano Man • Roundabout • Stairway to Heaven • Take the Long Way Home • and more.
00196019 Piano Solo.................................$14.99

CHRISTMAS CAROLS
Away in a Manger • Deck the Hall • The First Noel • God Rest Ye Merry, Gentlemen • Hark! the Herald Angels Sing • It Came upon the Midnight Clear • Jingle Bells • Joy to the World • O Holy Night • Silent Night • Up on the Housetop • We Three Kings of Orient Are • What Child Is This? • and more.
00147214 Piano Solo.................................$14.99

CHRISTMAS COLLECTION
Blue Christmas • The Christmas Song (Chestnuts Roasting on an Open Fire) • Frosty the Snow Man • Here Comes Santa Claus (Right down Santa Claus Lane) • Let It Snow! Let It Snow! Let It Snow! • Silver Bells • Sleigh Ride • White Christmas • Winter Wonderland • and more.
00172042 Piano Solo.................................$14.99

CLASSIC ROCK
Another One Bites the Dust • Aqualung • Beast of Burden • Born to Be Wild • Carry on Wayward Son • Layla • Owner of a Lonely Heart • Roxanne • Smoke on the Water • Sweet Emotion • Takin' It to the Streets • 25 or 6 to 4 • Welcome to the Jungle • and more!
00138517 Piano Solo.................................$14.99

Prices, contents, and availability subject to change without notice.

DISNEY FAVORITES
Beauty and the Beast • Can You Feel the Love Tonight • Chim Chim Cher-ee • For the First Time in Forever • How Far I'll Go • Let It Go • Mickey Mouse March • Remember Me (Ernesto de la Cruz) • You'll Be in My Heart • You've Got a Friend in Me • and more.
00283318 Piano Solo.................................$14.99

JAZZ POP SONGS
Don't Know Why • I Just Called to Say I Love You • I Put a Spell on You • Just the Way You Are • Killing Me Softly with His Song • Mack the Knife • Michelle • Smooth Operator • Sunny • Take Five • What a Wonderful World • and more.
00195426 Piano Solo.................................$14.99

JAZZ STANDARDS
All the Things You Are • Beyond the Sea • Georgia on My Mind • In the Wee Small Hours of the Morning • The Lady Is a Tramp • Like Someone in Love • A Nightingale Sang in Berkeley Square • Someone to Watch Over Me • That's All • What'll I Do? • and more.
00283317 Piano Solo.................................$14.99

POP BALLADS
Against All Odds (Take a Look at Me Now) • Bridge over Troubled Water • Fields of Gold • Hello • I Want to Know What Love Is • Imagine • In Your Eyes • Let It Be • She's Got a Way • Total Eclipse of the Heart • You Are So Beautiful • Your Song • and more.
00195425 Piano Solo.................................$14.99

POP HITS
Billie Jean • Fields of Gold • Get Lucky • Happy • Ho Hey • I'm Yours • Just the Way You Are • Let It Go • Poker Face • Radioactive • Roar • Rolling in the Deep • Royals • Smells like Teen Spirit • Viva la Vida • Wonderwall • and more.
00138156 Piano Solo.................................$14.99

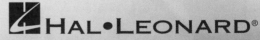

www.halleonard.com